MW01004238

MASKS
& HOW TO
MAKE THEM

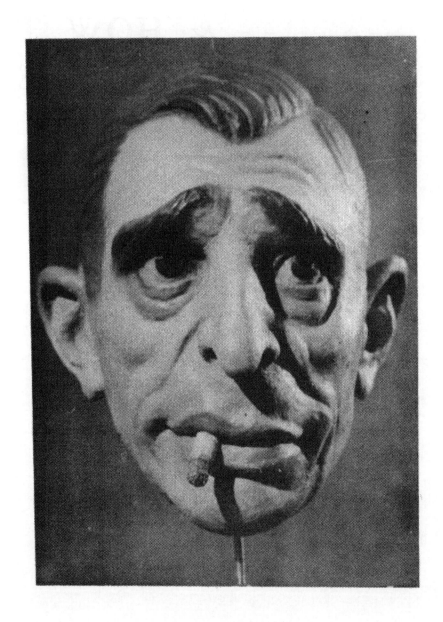

Some paper bags, a newspaper,
a little paint . . . . and this:

MASKS
& HOW TO MAKE THEM

by

Doane Powell

Published by BRIDGMAN PUBLISHERS, INC.
Pelham, New York

All masks shown were made by the author, also the photographs unless otherwise indicated. Thanks and acknowledgements are given to those photographers whose identity has not been established and whose work is labeled "No imprint". All likeness masks were made from photographs. Portrait masks indicate the additional help of a sitting from life. Most of the male masks modeled were photographed with a Rolleiflex camera equipped with delayed action. Strictly speaking these masks are not papier-mache. They are known as laminated paper masks.

TABLE OF CONTENTS

TO ALL THOSE GOOD PEOPLE
WHO HAVE SO KINDLY EN-
COURAGED ME, THIS BOOK
IS GRATEFULLY DEDICATED.

F O R E W O R D

You, too, can make masks.

Masks are fun. They can also be taken seriously.

In itself a mask is an ornament. The photograph of a mask makes an interesting picture; but a mask worn, with movement, by the proper person, becomes a Living Art.

Some of the happiest moments of one's life are often spent in creating something with the hands. Students in art, dramatic and other schools, colleges and universities and just plain people interested in arts and crafts will get a kick out of creating and reproducing mask personalities. The pleasure does not end with the making of masks. They are worn over and over again, used with different gestures, put on different heads and made the center of different actions and situations. They are a never ending source of entertainment.

The earliest known masks were made for ceremonial and ritualistic purposes. As expressions of the primitive mentality, as products of an escapist or creative instinct, they are abiding works of art and contributions to science. Anything we might do in imitation of these would be less than second rate. We have not the inspiration of the primitive gods to fire us. In this manual we will attempt no historic survey of mask making and psychological analysis. We will just try to be ourselves as of today, make a product of our own time, learn something interesting, and have fun.

The modern theatrical mask has been brought to a high degree of development. When worn, both these and the primitives require special costumes to be at their best. Obviously when worn with present day clothes they appear incongruous.

We wish here to concentrate on masks that can be worn with our ordinary present day clothing.

Our language gives us no word to express the difference between the non-wearable and wearable mask. Methods outlined here can be used to make either.

The use of bronze, marble or plaster requires knowledge only of form. The paper mask calls for not only a knowledge of form but also the effect of color on that form. Color is sometimes almost as important as form. Red hair, for example, may be more noticeable and characteristic in identifying a head than the shape of a nose or chin. Semi-caricature of some feature may be more recognizable than a photographic likeness.

The human face has few features: a pair of eyes and eyebrows, nose, mouth, ears, cheeks, jowls, chin, hairline, forehead, growth or absence of hair. Yet faces differ greatly in color and form. There is the full gamut of passive and prospective affections: pleasure and pain, content and discontent, relief and aggravation, wit and sadness. Add different lighting effects; a variety of costumes;

Portrait mask of O. O. McIntyre
Made for Cosmopolitan magazine

Portrait of Mrs. M. C. E.
of Norwich, N. Y.

consider the characteristic movements and tricks of manner of the living person who wears the mask—and the field of mask making becomes still wider, more alive and more fascinating.

The appeal of the mask is based on the almost universal failing that everyone likes to read faces. The subject matter is of paramount interest to the layman. While masks seem to have an almost universal appeal, their fans may be divided roughly into three groups:

GROUP I

This group prefers the grotesque—broad characterizations. It seems sometimes that the uglier and more violent the character portrayed, the greater the attraction.

GROUP II

This is composed of people who want to be pleased by beauty or mere prettiness. Nothing else attracts them.

GROUP III

For these, by far the largest group, the likeness or portrait mask is the most popular . . . perhaps because of its ability to recognize public personages flatters its vanity.

There should be illustrations here shown to satisfy each group.

There is beauty, character or significance in every face. To the artist and the student there is never any question of perpetuating the ordinary. In crowds on streets, in street-cars, buses and trains, in fact everywhere, we see many apparently totally-undistinguished faces. Yet, if we look deep enough, each face is fascinating. Even when it is vacant there is a reason for it.

The art of the mask described here is in its infancy: the mask that is lived with, not used merely in dramatic display, or hung upon the wall. Its practical place in everyday life has only just been touched.

Your imagination will evolve many ideas where the mask can be used. The present day mask should attract a following and command the respect it deserves.

Naturally the beginner wishes to make as few mistakes as possible. It is suggested that he begin with a miniature model before attempting something more ambitious. In the following pages he will be taken step by step through the processes by which the masks herein shown have been constructed. Individual ingenuity will supply better devices and short cuts. Added knowledge acquired from experience will suggest improvements.

Good luck to you. . . . Let's go!

HALF-MASK. Real eyeglass frames. Natural from moustache down.

THE BASE

The advantage of using a rigid base on which to model a mask is evident. The base serves as a guide for size, is easier to handle and saves expensive clay.

The simplest form of base is advisable for the beginner. The more closely the measurements of the base approach the actual head measurements the less clay is necessary. It is obvious that the base must not extend beyond the facial or cranial measurements.

The hat size will not tell the size of the facial area or indicate whether a mask will eventually fit the head. Very small or very large heads call for a different consideration and demand more careful and exact measurements.

No mask will fit everyone and as an average sized mask can be worn by more people we therefore plan a base for an average sized head or mask.

Perhaps the simplest mask base is made of plaster-of-paris about ½ inch thick in the form of an oval shell and flat on the bottom, like the cut-off top of a derby hat.

HOW TO MAKE A PLASTER BASE

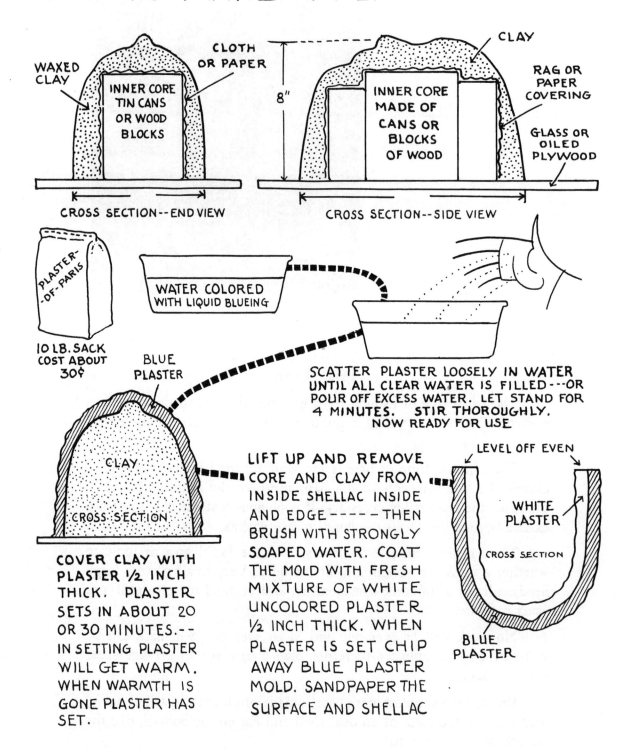

WAXED CLAY

INNER CORE TIN CANS OR WOOD BLOCKS

CLOTH OR PAPER

CROSS SECTION -- END VIEW

CLAY

8"

INNER CORE MADE OF CANS OR BLOCKS OF WOOD

RAG OR PAPER COVERING

GLASS OR OILED PLYWOOD

CROSS SECTION -- SIDE VIEW

PLASTER-OF-PARIS

10 LB. SACK COST ABOUT 30¢

WATER COLORED WITH LIQUID BLUEING

SCATTER PLASTER LOOSELY IN WATER UNTIL ALL CLEAR WATER IS FILLED---OR POUR OFF EXCESS WATER. LET STAND FOR 4 MINUTES. STIR THOROUGHLY. NOW READY FOR USE

BLUE PLASTER

CLAY

CROSS SECTION

COVER CLAY WITH PLASTER ½ INCH THICK. PLASTER SETS IN ABOUT 20 OR 30 MINUTES.-- IN SETTING PLASTER WILL GET WARM. WHEN WARMTH IS GONE PLASTER HAS SET.

LIFT UP AND REMOVE CORE AND CLAY FROM INSIDE SHELLAC INSIDE AND EDGE - - - - - THEN BRUSH WITH STRONGLY SOAPED WATER. COAT THE MOLD WITH FRESH MIXTURE OF WHITE UNCOLORED PLASTER ½ INCH THICK. WHEN PLASTER IS SET CHIP AWAY BLUE PLASTER MOLD. SANDPAPER THE SURFACE AND SHELLAC

LEVEL OFF EVEN

WHITE PLASTER

CROSS SECTION

BLUE PLASTER

To build a plaster base lay out a sheet of glass, oiled plywood or any flat surface and in the center place a can or blocks of wood, as a core on which to model the shape of the base. Over this foundation core, place strips of rag or paper on which to build the clay.

For measurements of the base follow those shown on the accompanying illustrations. The following measurements have been worked out for a base on which to model a mask for the AVERAGE sized head. On this base the clay is modeled close for a small head and thick for a larger one. Remember, the measurements are for the BASE and not for the mask itself.

Measurements

Male Head Base:
$5\frac{1}{2}$ inches side to side
$7\frac{1}{2}$ inches top to bottom
8 inches in depth

Female Head Base:
$4\frac{3}{4}$ inches side to side
7 inches top to bottom
8 inches in depth

Model the clay to the desired size and contour. To make a smooth surface sandpaper the clay, fill in all depressions, wipe with a soft cloth and burnish with the fingers.

Now, as a guide, mark a line from top to bottom in the center and from side to side, dividing the surface into quarters. Slightly below the intersection of the two lines and directly on the vertical line build up a short ridge to act as a guide when you later model the nose.

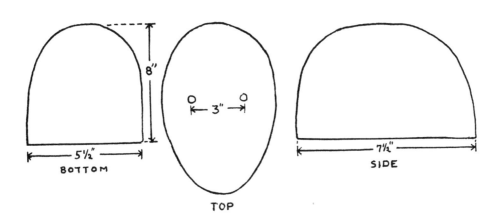

BOTTOM

TOP

SIDE

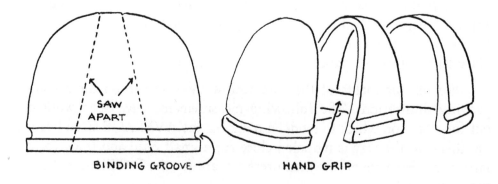

SAW APART

BINDING GROOVE

HAND GRIP

On the horizontal line make two depressions on each side of the center to indicate the eye sockets. Now on the center horizontal line make two holes in the clay with the flat end of a pencil three inches apart . . . that is 1½ inches each side of the center. These two holes will later hold plugs around which the clay will be modeled to insure that the eyes are in the correct place to be seen through.

Now, following the directions in the illustration, cover the clay with a layer of plaster ½ inch thick. This plaster should be colored with liquid bluing. When the plaster has set, turn it upside down and remove the entire center of filler blocks and clay.

The blue plaster shell now becomes your mold. Shellac the entire surface and edge. It will dry quickly. When dry, brush thoroughly the inside and edge with soapy water or stearic acid dissolved in kerosene, sometimes called coal oil.

Now mix a new batch of white, uncolored plaster and with it coat the inside of the mold ½ inch thick. Smooth off level with the edge of the blue mold.

When the plaster has set, chip away the blue mold with a cold chisel or knock it off with a blunt instrument directing the blows away from the center. If the inside of the mold has been well soaped the blue plaster should come off in well sized chunks. When all the blue mold has been removed the remaining white shell is your base. Sandpaper and shellac it.

The simple one-piece base described above is sometimes difficult to handle when later it has to be removed from the clay after drying the paper. It must be coaxed out carefully with the fingers. It can be done, but it is better to convert this simple base into a sectional base of three pieces making the removal operation much easier.

To make this sectional base, paste strings on the cast to indicate where sawing is to be done. Following the string guide, pencil in on the cast where the saw is to cut. Make the center section in the shape of a wedge, narrower towards the top, as shown in the illustration. Before sawing, cut a groove or notches around the base towards the bottom to act as a hold for a cord to bind the three sections together. Now saw the sections apart.

For further convenience in removal of the center wedge it is best to construct a handle across the bottom of the center wedge from one end to the other. This will give added stability. To do this, stand the wedge on its two ends on a flat surface and model a plaster bridge between them. To insure that the fresh plaster will stick to the already-set plaster of the mold, wet thoroughly the places where it will meet. If the plaster has become dry, paint it with shellac.

The surfaces, where sawed apart, should be sandpapered smooth. Now shellac the entire mold.

*   *   *   *

An excellent base may be made from a hat model block. One can often be picked up at a second hand store for very little. Cut down the sides all around to give a slight slope and remove all undercuts. An undercut is any projection that will interfere with the withdrawal of the base from the clay.

A professional base. Two of the four sides have been removed showing the central core, base and grooves.

A professional base can be made by a manufacturer of hat model forms. This base has a central core or foundation. Around the central core are four sides that slide in grooves so that the entire four sides can be lifted up at once. The four sides then collapse giving easy access to the clay.

This is an expensive job and there are but few manufacturers that can make it, and these are found only in the largest of our cities.

*　　*　　*　　*

Of course the ideal guide for a base is a life mask. Warning is given that it is dangerous for an amateur or novice to attempt to make a life mask, unless he has the most careful supervision. Most sculptors and some art schools instructors possess the experience necessary to superintend this type of work.

Portrait mask of
Frank J. Black
Music Director for N.B.C.

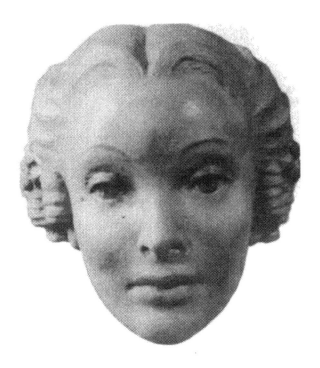

Two-toned formalized head.

MODELING

The creative and most interesting part of mask making comes in the modeling. The mask itself may be likened to an outer shell or skin which tightly covers the underlying bones and muscles. A structure to reveal the bones and muscles must be modeled. Thus the mask maker is first of all a sculptor and his success depends on his ability to create types that are both interesting in character and significant in structure.

The tendency of most beginners and those who have studied drawing or painting on flat surfaces, is not to appreciate the third dimension or depth of a face. They too often refer to the profile, not realizing that if the planes of the different forms are in right relation to each other, the profile will take care of itself. The outline or profile changes at every move. The masses in relation to each other do not.

Tools

Your fingers are your best tools.

Regular modeling tools of course are desirable but not entirely necessary. A knife, hair pins or bent wire will do very well. Medium and fine sandpaper and a soft cloth completes the outfit for this portion of the process.

17

The Medium

Throughout this book the designation or word, "clay" refers to that non-hardening wax-like composition usually used in kindergartens. It comes under such trade names as Plastaline, Plastacine, Modelette, Plastalina, Plastacina, etc. These clays usually come in different degrees of hardness. The harder grades are preferable for mask modeling as harder tamping with the stencil brush can be done on its surface when the paper is applied.

Clay improves with age and use, and may be used over and over again. If the base is large, about four pounds of clay should be enough.

Modeling

Before actually beginning manipulating the clay you will find it advisable to claw some soft soap into your fingernails. Soap, however, has very little effect in removing clay from your hands. Boraxo is excellent for this, as is also mechanic's soap. You will find clay very "tracky" if any of it gets on the floor, so, if you value your rugs, be careful.

Before applying clay be sure that the base is covered with loose strips of cloth or paper toweling. If this is not done, the clay will stick to the base and it will be practically impossible to remove the base later.

The best light under which to work should come slightly from above. The importance of viewing your work from all angles, above, underneath and from the sides, as it progresses, cannot be too greatly

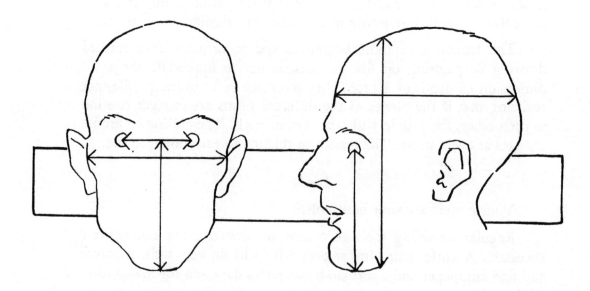

Main points to be measured in estimating size and fit of mask.

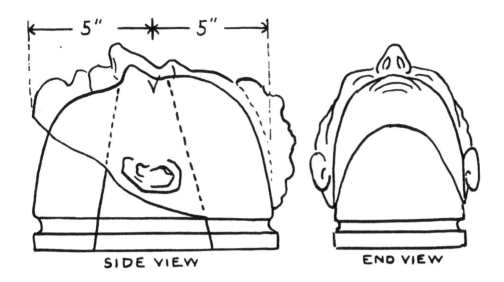

SIDE VIEW   END VIEW

stressed. It is also advisable to take the model into different lights and check up your modeling by holding it in front of a mirror to see it in reverse. When finished, the forms should look right from any angle and in any light.

Remember that the finished mask will not be an exact replica of your modeling, as in working for a plaster of paris reproduction.

Three layers of paper are to be superimposed over the clay so you must allow for compensations. The modeling itself may be sharp and clean cut, but the layers of paper will modify and soften all the sharpnesses and fill out the hollows.

Caricature everything slightly. Don't be afraid to exaggerate. The paper will minimize it all. Model the creases deeper than you want them to appear in the mask itself. The paper will fill them in. Make the eye-openings slightly larger and the nostril openings somewhat wider. It is these allowances the mask sculptor makes, that makes the work from that of other sculptors different.

Check up on your modeling by looking at it from above and beneath to see the roundness of form and that the eyes are in the same plane. Indicate the pupils of the eyes for the proper expression. Later, before papering, the pupils of the eyes should be filled in and the surface of the eyeball rounded.

The two sides of the face are never exactly alike. One side slopes back more quickly than the other. Eyes are not the same size. Be sure and feel the roundness of the eyeballs underneath the lids. One side of the mouth slopes up or down in relation to the eye line. Some noses point slightly left or right. Ears are placed forward or back, high or low on the skull. The general angle of the ear has a tendency to take the same slant as the nose placement. There are exceptions of course, but remember that the mask when worn stands away from the face so that an area in back of the ears should be allowed to hide the ears of the wearer.

It is obvious that a mask has to be slightly larger than the wearer's head or it cannot be worn. The snugger the fit, the better. A mask too large for the wearer looks out of proportion to the neck and body and the effect is lost. Therefore, in modeling, have in mind the proportions of the eventual wearer.

A mask of average size allows for more people being able to wear it, while a very large or a very small mask confines the wearing of it to a very few. The hat size gives no indication of the width of the face. Measurements should be made from a point just in front of the ears on the cheek bones, and the height of the eye line measured from just underneath the chin.

In putting a finish on your modeling the burnishing with your fingers is apt to ridge up the clay. To get a smooth finish, take some medium sandpaper and pass over the surface. This will show up the hollows that are not noticeable to the naked eye. Fill in the depressions, sandpaper over again and wipe with a soft cloth. Go over the surface again with some fine sandpaper, soft-cloth again and burnish lightly with the fingers. For an extremely high finish, dip your fingers in water before rubbing the clay.

In modeling your clay, work slightly beyond the areas to be papered on the back of the head, behind the ears and underneath the jaws.

In character heads, dare to be original. Don't be afraid.

There is a personal satisfaction or triumph in creating a new face that conveys character.

In likeness or portrait masks, the important thing is that one must study the essential parts of the face that makes it different from others. While the character head calls for creativeness and originality, the likeness mask demands keen analysis. It also has its limitations. To sound something like Gertrude Stein: "if a likeness is not a likeness it is not a likeness." If a nose is not interesting you call attention to it if you make it so.

Some faces are fascinating due to vivacity. In repose the face may be less than interesting. A smile can transform an ordinary face into something altogether charming.

Many faces are not susceptible to caricature try as you will.

Remember your limitations: the mask is to be worn: the eyeholes are to be seen through.

When you are completely satisfied with your modeled clay, viewed it from all angles and in different lights, then and only 'til then, are you ready for the next step which is, PAPERING.

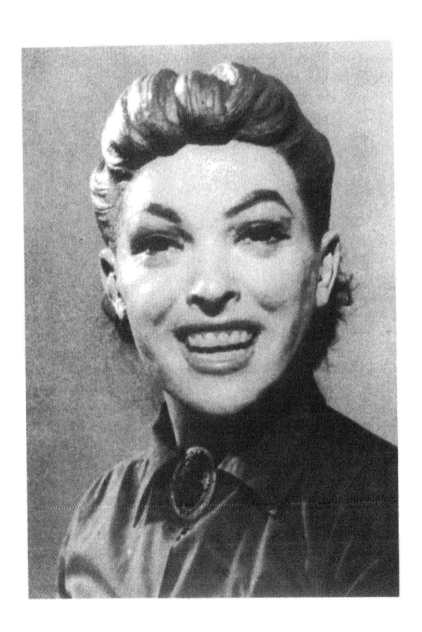

SMILE ANATOMY

Look in the mirror. Hold a pencil horizontally in front of the mouth in repose. Then smile. See how the mouth line is raised, especially at the corners. Note that this shortens the upper lip, up and down, as it flattens itself against the teeth. Study the difference between a smile with the lips closed and a grin with the teeth exposed. The nostrils are raised and widened. Some noses are slightly flattened.

In a smile the muscles extending from the upper part of the nostrils to the sides of the mouth are bunched up. Make the eyes smile with the mouth. The cheek muscles press upwards and bunch up the eye muscles. If the eyes do not conform with the smile, the result will be a professional or toothpaste smile.

ADHESIVES

Lest some one might think the term adhesive means adhesive tape, we announce at once that adhesive in this type of work is glue, mucilage, rubber cement, paste, or anything that will make one surface stick to another.

Ordinary glue can be used for decorative or rigid masks. Glue, however, dries brittle and is not suitable for the wearable mask, which must have a certain amount of flexibility. For experimental purposes library paste is good enough. It is made from dextrine with glycerine added to keep it moist. A mask made with library paste softens and loses its shape when exposed to heat. It is therefore impracticable for a durable mask and dextrine instead is suggested.

There are dozens of dextrines having different properties. Some can be used only with cold water, others with hot. It is therefore inadvisable to ask simply for "dextrine." You are safe if you stipulate tapioca dextrine. It costs a little more but is more glutinous than the others.

Here is the way to handle dextrine ample enough for one mask. The formula is one part dextrine to one part water. Bring ½ cup of water to boil. Turn off the heat and add ½ cup of dextrine. Stir thoroughly. Crush any lumps with a spatula, back of a spoon or palette knife.

For additional strength add a small quantity of glue or casein glue. If a larger amount of the mixture is required a drop or two of formaldehyde or oil-of-cloves will keep it sweet.

23

As it cools, a thick film will form on the surface. Stir this into the mixture until it is dissolved. When entirely cooled the adhesive is ready to use. If left for a matter of hours it will eventually jell. When not in use and in a state of jell a little water poured on the surface, and not stirred in, will keep the mixture in good condition for days. Especially in warm weather. Pour the water off when used again. One pound of dextrine is enough for a dozen masks.

Adhesives of flour paste and wall paper paste have been used but satisfactory results are not guaranteed. Rubber cement for patching is also inadvisable for permanency.

FILLERS

After drying the wet paper, in constructing a mask, small crevices or rough spots will appear. A small piece of gummed paper pasted over the weak spot will sometimes be sufficient for a patch. Smaller crevices are often left to be filled in later with the first or priming coat of paint.

Plastic wood is used in reinforcing or holding in place wire for moustaches. Use in small quantities only as it is apt to shrink and come away from point of contact.

Casein water paint makes a good filler. It dries waterproof.

Make your workmanship as perfect as possible. The less filling and patching you do the better.

Note that the hair on top of the head is of paper. Since the wearer's hair is of the same color, it is shown hanging in back.

25

Experiments in facial types and expressions

This comic strip character made entirely from newspaper

Impractical
Eyes too high

Glum faced characters are not as popular as smiling ones. They are best as foils for beauty

26

Make hairdo appropriate to facial character

A good sample of a toothy smile

27

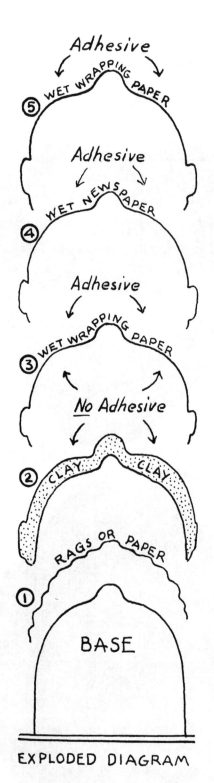

Adhesive

⑤ WET WRAPPING PAPER

Adhesive

④ WET NEWSPAPER

Adhesive

③ WET WRAPPING PAPER

No Adhesive

② CLAY   CLAY

RAGS OR PAPER

① BASE

EXPLODED DIAGRAM

EARS

The center of the ears is the pivotal point for the movement of the head up and down. Whether large or small, the ears are usually placed between lines running horizontally from the eyebrows and the bottom of the nose. The ears usually take the same general slant of the nose, although there are many queer exceptions. In non-likeness masks it is permissible to place the ears slightly low to give the effect of a larger skull area, thus giving a more youthful appearance. So, also, if the ears are placed higher, older age is indicated by making the skull smaller in relation to the facial area.

PAPER AND PAPERING

Commercial listings carry some 208 brands of paper. It is necessary to go into technicalities only to show reasons for arriving at the choice of papers suitable to the fabrication of masks.

If you have the novice's idea that thin paper is desirable, forget it. It has no tensile strength and can not be handled when wet.

Paper is usually made of woodpulp, rags and old paper. For masks the unbleached woodpulp paper is best. Bleaching weakens tensile strength, and high grade finished papers have a casein filler which retards water penetration.

Our first choice therefore is the Kraft group of wrapping papers. Next in value comes newsprint paper. Printed newspapers will serve, but without impregnation of adhesives they become brittle, lose strength and turn yellow with age. Impregnation means the filling in between the fibres so as to bind them more closely together.

Wrapping papers are manufactured in varying weights. The lighter weights of Kraft paper used for small grocery bags serve our purpose the best. Heavier qualities are used for reinforcing areas that demand additional strength. Keep away from glossy surfaced papers.

It is inadvisable to use layer upon layer of the same kind or color of paper because, when wet, it is difficult to judge whether the entire surface has been covered. Thin spots weaken the structure.

A mask can be made entirely of newspaper or newsprint paper: but experience has shown that alternating layers of newsprint and wrapping paper produces a sturdier mask. If newsprint is used entirely, blank sheets are of course preferable; if printed pages are more conveniently at hand, select those that are the least heavily inked. Want ad sections are the best, with a center layer of color print to make sure the entire surface is evenly covered.

Preparation

Thoroughly soak all paper in water. TEAR, DO NOT CUT, in strips about 3 x 6 inches. Lay these in separately and cross them so that no double thicknesses occur. This will guarantee that two strips will not adhere without the necessary adhesive between them. A double thickness of paper will form air spots between the layers when dried and weaken the structure.

Heavy wrapping paper needs more soaking than lighter weight paper. It should be immersed, taken out, squeezed, rumpled and replaced in the water. An hour's soaking will do.

Soak newspaper for an hour at least or until thoroughly water-logged. It will not stand squeezing or rumpling.

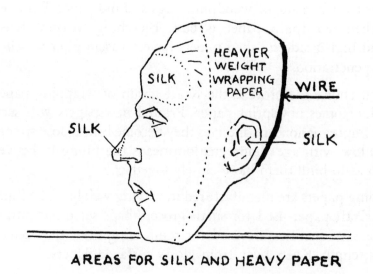

AREAS FOR SILK AND HEAVY PAPER

How to Apply the Paper

When you apply paper to the clay you will need 3 brushes: a stencil brush for tamping large areas; a smaller brush for crevices; and a large, flat brush for spreading on the adhesive. If a long-haired stencil brush is used stretch a rubber band around the bristles about half way up to prevent the bristles from spreading. This will also give a certain spring to the operation.

First Layer

Apply the first layer of paper wet WITHOUT adhesive. Tamp it down with the stencil brush strip by strip on the clay until you have removed all wrinkles and air bubbles. Tear small bits of the wet paper to apply around the eyes, ears and nostrils. EACH PIECE MUST OVERLAP TO INSURE FULL COVERAGE.

Second Layer

Spread adhesive on the first layer. On top of this tamp down the second layer. For this second layer bits of silk can be pasted, not tamped, on the smooth surfaces of the brow, chin, end of nose and especially the ears. The ears because they are thin and stick out cannot take much tamping. Silk has a tendency to draw while drying and is not used in creases or hollows. Silk from discarded slips, underwear or nightgowns is best. The thin material of stockings has no strength. Heavier silks are hard to impregnate with adhesives. Grades of nylon, celanese and rayon may also be used.

Heavy, thick wrapping paper is used for reinforcement on the top of the head, around the edges in back and underneath the jaw and chin. These areas get the hardest wear and help keep the more fragile parts in position.

Third Layer

The third layer of wrapping paper is applied in the same manner as the second layer except that, after application, it should be thoroughly smeared with adhesive. Rub or burnish with your fingers to make sure all parts adhere.

During the entire operation of papering never allow the paper to become dry. If your work is done in an especially dry atmosphere keep it wrapped in moist rags when it is not being worked on. Two or three layers of wet cloths are necessary if it is left overnight or for a matter of hours.

THE MASK IS NOW READY FOR DRYING.

Two photographs of the same mask. On the left crepe hair has been superimposed on the paper hair seen above.

32

Here crepe hair gives a softening effect to the outline. Ugly
masks make a foil, by contrast, for good looking ones.

ANIMAL HEADS

Animal heads, as a rule, are not satisfactory. This is due mainly to the fact that the eyes of most animals are far apart and in a mask it is almost impossible to see through them.

Naturally animal heads do not fit the head easily or go with the human figure. They are primarily meant for children's entertainment and the occasions are so infrequent that they are hardly worth while.

The monkey's head here shown was made for a laugh. Long necked or very large animals are out. Some short, snubnosed dogs are possible, but even these cannot be seen through readily.

GRAY-O REILLY

Stylized head fabricated for Harpers Bazaar

DRYING AND FINISHING

There are several ways to dry wet paper while on the clay form. It depends a great deal on the season of the year or climate. In summertime place in the sun. Turn occasionally so that all sides are exposed, in the meanwhile burnishing the paper with the fingers or a spatula. By burnishing is meant the rubbing of the outer surface with a smooth surfaced instrument. This burnishing hardens the surface, removes roughnesses and assures the different layers of paper being welded into a solid whole.

In the wintertime or indoors, use a hair dryer, an electric fan, an electric reflector heater or radiator. In drying be sure not to overheat. The waxy clay will melt and adhere to the paper.

It is important not to remove the clay until the paper is entirely dried through and through. If removed before the paper is hard the clay is likely to stick to the paper and buckle it.

Now, while the dry paper is still on the base, make repairs or alterations. Difficulties will be encountered if they are made after the paper has become oily from painting. It is evident proper adhesion can not be made if the paper is oily.

Sandpaper the surface where a high finish is desired; as for example to portray a smooth, shiny forehead. If a major alteration is necessary cut the offending portion, remodel the part underneath, and paper over.

In removing hard or curled-up paper a good instrument is made by dividing in two parts a double edged safety razor blade. This makes the blade safer to handle. For fine incisions break off one end of the half blade at an angle with pliers. This leaves a very fine point.

Now pencil in the eyes. Hold the mask up to a mirror and check on size and matching. Draw the pupils in and with a sharp pointed instrument pierce the pupils and enlarge them by inserting the end of a rat-tail file and twisting it to the desired enlargement and to a uniform depth.

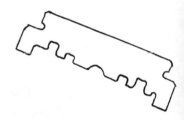

In removing the mask from the base turn it upside down, holding it between the knees and gently but firmly wangle the base out. Sometimes better results are to be had by holding the base firmly to the floor and lifting the clay and paper off. At this stage is shown the importance of covering the base foundation with cloth rags or paper before applying the clay. Also the importance of having no undercuts or rough surfaces.

Remove the cloth or paper next to the clay. Then remove the clay. The thinner portions are easily removed. The thicker portions are removed piece by piece with the fingers or with the help of some fairly blunt instrument. In removing the clay from the ears and nose care must be taken not to use a sharp instrument. It is apt to pierce the thin paper.

After all the clay has been removed hold the mask against a strong light and from in back check up on spots that are too thin or perhaps have been punctured. Patch these places with pieces of gummed paper. Try mask on head to assure that it fits before trimming the back edges.

With sharp scissors or razor blade, trim the rough edged paper on the back and cut out the extra paper inside the nostrils with long handled manicure scissors.

Bind the back edges with gummed paper. Gummed paper comes in different widths. Cut what you have cross or lengthwise into strips about 2 x ¾ inches. For further rigidity gum-tape a piece of No. 20 rustproof wire along the upper edge from ear to ear. This retains the curve and prevents the mask from getting out of shape and sagging when it is hung up for any length of time. This wire is obtainable in most hardware and 5 and 10¢ stores.

The paper may be painted on direct. It is better, however, to strengthen the surface by painting or blowing on a thin coating of lacquer. To spray use a spray gun also bought at most hardware and 10¢ stores.

After using a spray gun clean the stem with a pipe cleaner or the lacquer will clog it up. Lacquer dries in about 10 minutes. Do NOT use shellac. Shellac dries brittle and shiny and as a rule leaves no tooth for the oil paint brush.

THE MASK IS NOW READY FOR PAINTING.

Duplications of masks is possible by cutting the paper with a razor blade. Cut from points near outer end of eyebrows to in back of ears; from the widow's peak to back of head; from nostrils to underneath ears; from center of chin to throat.

The removal of the paper will destroy the nose and ears but these can easily be reconstructed.

After the paper has been wangled off the razor cuts are bound together, front and back, with gummed paper. All this makes for a weaker and structurally inferior mask as compared to the solid one-piece mask, and is not advised.

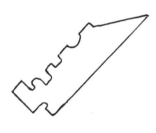

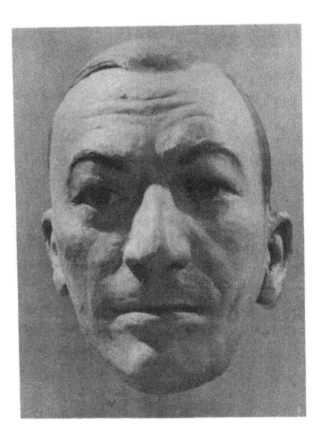

Portrait mask of NOEL COWARD
made from one sitting

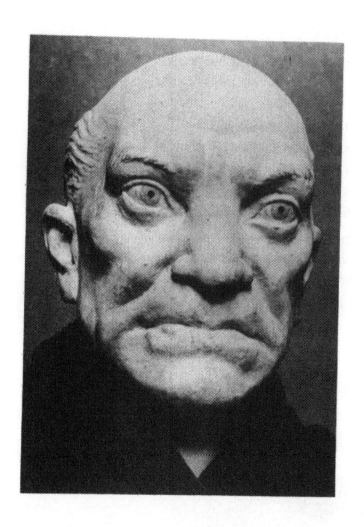

Character mask before painting. The surface is newsprint paper. The eyes have been tinted in for placement. The pupils are formed with a rat-tail file while still on the clay.

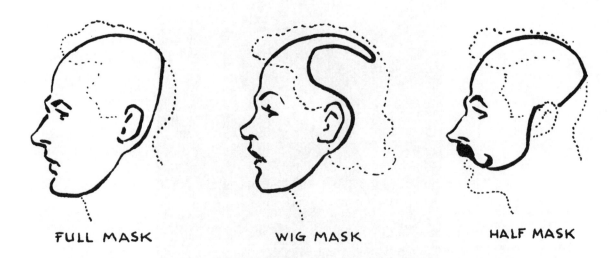

FULL MASK   WIG MASK   HALF MASK

PAINTING THE MASK

The first consideration in painting a mask is that it should look equally well in daylight and by artificial light. If anything, it should be painted to look better under artificial light since that is most often used. It is under a half-light that a mask looks most convincing.

Masks can be painted with tempera colors: but we are concerned with the wearable mask and obviously with wearing and handling it is quickly soiled. Oil paint is therefore better since it is easy to clean with a moist cloth and is more durable.

A mask should be neither shiny nor chalky. Avoid monotony of color. The following suggestions are the product of many years of trial and error. They may save a lot of grief:

Colors

Let's discuss colors first . . . then the methods of applying them. Not all the colors listed are necessary for any one mask. A much simpler list of colors may be used but the list given below should fill every need.

White:

Zinc white ground in japan. This is a quick drying white and therefore good for a first filler coat. It is apt to turn yellow and darken with age and may affect the over painting.

Striping White: A smoother japan white. It dries mat and has better coverage.

Zinc White: Being an oil paint it dries shiny. This can be offset in some degree by the ample use of turpentine.

The ideal paint has been a Mussini Mat White made in Germany but unobtainable for the present.

Black:

Ivory Black ground in japan. Ordinary oil blacks are very slow driers. Japan black dries quickly, is good for painting eyes and hair. It dries mat but can be made shiny and darker by coats of varnish.

Red:

Poster Red ground in japan. This dries quickly and may darken later. It is excellent for an under painting.

Other Colors:

Vermillion	Terre Verte	Burnt Sienna
Light Red	Raw Umber	Alizarine Crimson
	Van Dyke Brown	

Application

While painting a mask it is best to be in bright daylight near a window to insure accuracy: but the effects should be checked under artificial light. Colored walls influence the color of your paint. A mask painted in a room with yellowish walls will look entirely too yellow when seen in daylight.

Formulas given here are not inflexible. They are but little more than a guide for persons who are unfamiliar with oil paint as a medium.

If a mask is made for photographic reproduction it is advisable to use slightly darker shades than normal. It is necessary in selecting flesh tones to choose something halfway between winter bleach and summer tan. No one mask can be colored suitably to fit both conditions at the same time.

In painting a female mask the first color used is Japan Red to form the lips. This serves as an underpainting which will show through later when the color is modified. The eyes at this time should be painted in dark for size and placement. Hold up before a mirror to see that the eyes track. Paint dark also the under side of the upper eye lids.

At least two coats of paint are necessary in painting. The first coat or filler is White with Burnt Sienna or Light Red mixed in. This gives a warm undertone. Mix enough to cover the entire facial area. The hair area may be gone over thinly by adding Black or Van Dyke Brown to the facial color. All this helps in estimating the final tonal value. The first coat will look disappointingly hard and monotonous. When almost dry the forehead is burnished with the fingers to give the effect of skin tightly stretched over bone. Now indicate the placement of the eyebrows.

We are now ready for the second painting. Variety should be striven for. Hold the mask beside your face in front of a mirror to judge whether the general tonal values shall be lightened or darkened.

Mix enough of the general skin tone desired. This general skin tone should be the base with which to mix your other colors to make the entire mask colors harmonious.

An acceptable general skin tone is composed of White with Burnt Sienna or Light Red modified with just a touch of Terre Verte to kill redness. This is known as the basic color. For men the Burnt Sienna should dominate; for women the Light Red.

For the feminine masks paint the entire face up to the eyes and well into the hairline border. For rouged areas add just a touch of Vermillion. Use this color for tops and lobes of ears. Underneath and over the eyes add a touch of Terre Verte or Raw Umber.

For masculine masks paint the base color up to the eyes, well into the hairline and shaving areas. Add a little Vermillion or Light Red for tops of ears and to the upper part of muscles running from the nose to the side of the mouth. Merge with fingers. Add Raw Umber for above and underneath the eyes. For the shaven area add a bit of Van Dyke Brown. If desired add just a suspicion of Alizarine Crimson for the end of the nose.

For feminine lips use straight Red, using your own judgment as to the shape desired. Masculine lips, not being lip-sticked in real life, call for an addition of Red or Light Red to the base color, the edges being soft and merged.

Teeth and eyeballs are painted first with Ivory Enamel or Japan White. This dries almost immediately and will look decidedly pronounced. Later this white base will shine through the over-coating and give a luminosity that is naturalistic. Hold a handkerchief or piece of white paper behind your teeth to see how low in tone they are compared to pure white.

The eyeballs are also lower in tone than you would at first imagine, due to the surrounding darks. For the color add White with a little Raw Umber or Raw Sienna. The upper part of the eyeballs are darkened slightly to simulate the shadow cast by eyelashes. The color edge on the upper lid should be soft. The upper portion of the under lid is slightly darker than the general skin tone. Darker coloration of the lower lid is soft and merged.

The color of the eyes themselves should be mixed in Japan White to obviate any shine. For blue eyes do not use straight Blue. Oftentimes Black, which is slightly bluish, mixed with White will be sufficient, with just a touch of Blue or Terre Verte. Most mannikin eyes are too blue, especially when seen in daylight. Remember to paint the inside edge of the cutout pupil a deep Black.

HAIR

The general skin tone helps indicate the desired tonal value of the hair. A straight solid color is advisable except in the graying towards the temples of an older person. The modeling of the hair gives enough variety to look natural. Positively avoid a sharp hairline.

The hair color is merged with the facial coloring while it is still wet, either with the fingers, a fine brush or by stippling. A sharp hairline will detract from the face and look hard and artificial. The eyebrows on a feminine mask as a rule are darker and more sharply defined than on a masculine one. Moustaches are also softened at the hair line.

For black hair Van Dyke Brown is more pleasing than Black. For reddish or auburn hair use Burnt Sienna or Light Red. For grey hair use White with an intermixture of Burnt Sienna and Green, or maybe Van Dyke Brown. For blondes use White with Raw Sienna.

After the paint has become thoroughly dry a little retouch varnish painted on the lips, teeth and eyeballs will give them a moist look and relieve the monotony of texture.

* * * *

The inside surface of the mask demands attention. All bits of clinging clay are removed by scraping. To preserve the inner surface and make it impervious to moisture the entire inside should be either painted with a coat of clear lacquer, ivory colored enamel, paint or varnish. This, when hard, gives an additional strength and prevents softening of the paper from perspiration. Enamel gives the best finish but adds slightly to the weight.

POOR, OLD, WORRIED UNCLE SAM

A very satisfactory mat surface may be obtained by mixing clear lacquer with ordinary oil paint. Pat off excess oil with a soft cloth when partially dry.

The mask opens up a new field in political campaigns both local and national. As a focal point at banquets or conventions where candidates can not be present a mask of the personage serves as a substitute.

There are many outlets for masks in night clubs, cocktail parties, movies, theatres and church benefits. Fashion shows, window displays, lectures and general entertainment are always calling for something different. The likeness or portrait mask has proved, by far, the most most popular in general public appeal.

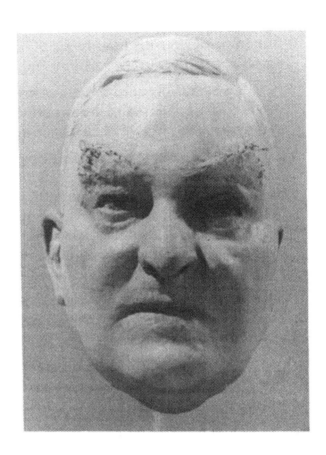

Ex-Vice Pres. Garner

ACCESSORIES

It is a maxim that a single medium be consistently used in any artistic endeavor. It is considered a confession of weakness when an artist goes outside his medium to complete his work. The making of a mask, however, creates a slightly different situation. Nothing is to be gained by making ear-rings or eyeglass frames out of paper—it is so much more practical to use real ones. They are inanimate objects anyway.

But, a questioner will ask, why not use glass eyes and real hair. The only answer is that you might as well consider wax figures as Art and dispense altogether with illusion and the human element. After all, Art is NOT realism. Art is the creating of the ILLUSION of reality.

Crepe Hair

In making masks crepe hair is sometimes helpful. From an artistic standpoint it might be considered a crutch. For advertising photography it is often necessary where the hardness of hair modeled out of paper is undesirable and softness of outline is.

Sometimes a mask is made of the facial area alone and a wig is superimposed over the head to keep the mask in place. A cheap theatrical wig, if obtainable, will serve this purpose.

Crepe hair, obtained from a wig maker or theatrical costumer, comes in long braids in almost any color of natural hair. There is enough hair in one braid to make quite a few formations.

When unravelled from the string which binds it the hair is very crinkly. To remove this crinkle comb out the hair, stretch and pass it back and forth in the steam from the spout of a kettle or coffee pot. When the hair is thoroughly stretched and softened by the steam fasten one end with a clothes pin or photo clasp and suspend with a weight at the other end. Leave stretched until dry. In this condition it is combed out as used.

To attach the hair to a mask it is possible to use ordinary glue if care is taken to keep it away from the hair line . . . since glue dries with an undesirable shine.

Wig makers use a collodian glue which dries dull almost immediately. It must be applied before the mask is painted, for it contains ether, which dissolves paint.

Care is needed to leave a natural hair line. The best suggestion is to attach the hair so that it may be folded forward and then turned back. In this way the hair juncture is hidden. Solvents for these glues are either lacquer thinner or acetone.

Hair groups are attached one over the other in a shingle formation following the natural hair growth direction. When finished the hair is slightly fixed by spraying with clear lacquer. Use bobby pins where necessary as in natural hair.

Sometimes discarded eyeglass frames can be used by removing the glass. Other cheap sunglasses will fill the bill. Being unable to procure these, or they do not suit your purpose, frames are made by bending wire and soldering on the side pieces, called templars. As masks are not meant to be looked at too closely these home made spectacles are very satisfactory and photograph well. It is best to attach frames firmly to the mask. This is done by sewing or wiring the templars back of the ears or at the sides of the nose piece.

Ear-rings are modeled if close to the ear but if hanging ear-rings are desired it is best to sew or wire real ear-rings on.

*   *   *   *

What is one to do with a mask when it is not being worn? Well, a mask may be packed away in a box or paper bag. It may be used as a wall ornament or displayed on a table or stand.

In displaying a mask the tilt or angle at which it is hung is most important. The entire effect of a mask may be spoiled if improperly hung. The inside of a mask is hard and slippery. It will slide around if hung on anything equally hard. To avoid this tack a strip of sponge rubber on the gadget which holds the mask. This will secure it at the desired angle and prevent it from sliding around.

Hat model stands make convenient racks. Also a hanger can be made by securing parts of a hat model fixture and constructing a hanger such as shown in accompanying illustration.

Wall surfaces or rays of light will show from behind through the openings of the eyes or mouth. To avoid this drape a black cloth over the hanger or paste black strips over the openings from in back.

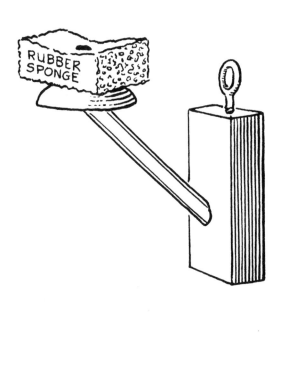

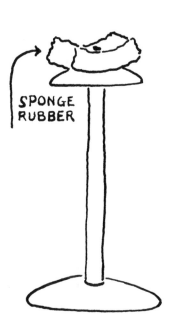

It is very important that a mask be hung at a proper angle. If improperly hung the correct impression will be entirely lost.

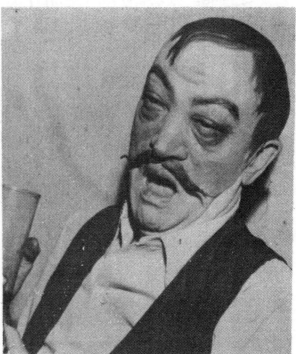

48   Three pictures taken from a full page spread in the New York World-Telegram. Upper picture
taken in Sheridan Square. Lower left: Caricature of John L. Lewis. Lower right: Character study
of a half-mask.

Mask of Mrs. Eleanor Roosevelt.

THESE MASKS CALL FOR APPROPRIATE COSTUMES

Chester Morris, movie star, wears his Powell
half-mask in his activities as a magician.

John Mulholland, internationally known master-
magician, in one of his two Powell masks.

THE HALF MASK

One drawback to the mask that covers the entire face is that, when worn, the actions of the wearer are confined entirely to pantomime. The half-mask overcomes this deficiency by allowing the wearer to talk and get over a message; to sing, whistle, laugh, grimace, drink or smoke. It is much more comfortable to wear. The mask covers more of the back of the head and the ears are exposed.

The half-mask, however, is relegated entirely to the masculine wearer. It eliminates the feminine, likeness and portrait mask.

The reason for this is that a half-mask demands a fairly large moustache to cover the transition from the upper rigid mask to the lower uncovered face of the wearer. The flexible muscles of mouth action need this covering to create illusion. A mask modeled to the mouth contour without the moustache has proved unsatisfactory.

Technically the half-mask has particular requirements. The base upon which the modeling is done practically demands a built-up life mask upon which to work. This will give the exact curvature of the mouth, cheeks and jaws for correct fitting. The method of papering, drying and painting is the same as for the whole-mask.

A life mask is made of plaster-of-paris by the plaster, Plastico Moulage or Negokol process. The life mask is tilted at an angle, built well back on the head and then a plaster base built up underneath as shown in the illustration.

The entire base is sawed apart into three sections, a V-shaped wedge being the center section with the small end at the top of the head. The end of the nose is cut away, two holes for the insertion of plugs to show eye location and the lower lip taken away. The cheeks are also sandpapered down to insure a perfect fit. A handle is constructed between the two ends of the center wedge to allow a convenient withdrawal of the wedge.

The sides or intersectional edges must be straight and smooth. Key wedges are constructed to prevent slipping. Grooves are cut to hold a heavy rubber band or cord passed around the lower part of the base to hold the three sections together. This groove is well underneath the paper areas so that it may be removed before the center wedge is taken out and the dry paper is removed. The two end sections are then removed to expose the clay.

Moustaches

The entire moustache is modeled. It is almost impossible to make the moustache entirely of paper. After the moustache is modeled, cut it off near its base before papering.

After the entire half-mask has been taken off its base, cut off the paper edges and insert wires at the curve desired and fix in place with plastic wood. Pieces of cotton or kapok are soaked in rubber cement or glue and modeled onto the wires to the desired size and shape.

In papering the paper should extend well back from in front of the ears. When finished, the mask is put on the head and the exact location of the ears penciled in, cut out and bound with gummed tape and wire.

The Barber Commuters Quartette wears half-masks at an Advertising Club of New York gathering.

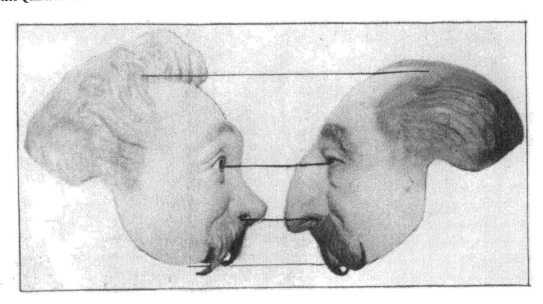

An experiment showing how small and how large a nose can be made, using the same head measurements.

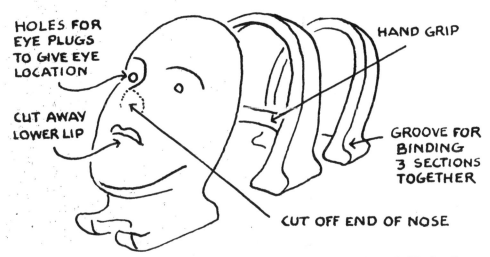

HOLES FOR EYE PLUGS TO GIVE EYE LOCATION

HAND GRIP

CUT AWAY LOWER LIP

GROOVE FOR BINDING 3 SECTIONS TOGETHER

CUT OFF END OF NOSE

HALF-MASK BASE SEPARATED TO SHOW 3 SECTIONS

53

Half-mask base showing three separate sections. Front section is an altered life-mask. Lower lip is cut away. End of nose is cut off. Holes in eyes for plugs to show exact location for visibility.

Thomas Alva Edison

*Two of seven celebrity masks made
for Pepsi-Cola publicity.*

54

Mark Twain

The Duke and Duchess of Windsor

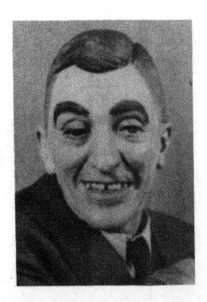

A gentleman from
Massachusetts

A section of an exhibition of the author's masks held in the Lotos Club Gallery, N. Y.

In this mask note that the lips have been varnished, and the upper parts of the eyeballs have been darkened to give the effect of shadows cast by long eyelashes.

The "beauty mask" is the hardest to achieve. It is rather futile and presumptuous to compete with real, living beauty. A mask expression is of necessity set.

Too often, in striving for perfection, symmetry or finish, one loses the spark of vitality. Not to decry the faultless it is far better to stop and retain the vigor of personality than to endeavor too far for finish and lose character or charm thereby.

Never show a character mask after showing a likeness or portrait one. The character mask will fall flat, no matter how good, as people will try to read a likeness into it and will be disappointed.

Claudette

A cocktail party models some early masks.

58

ADDENDA

Cleaning

In cleaning the painted surface of a mask avoid hot water or soap of any kind. As in oil painting one of the best methods of cleaning is to cut a raw potato and rub the cut side over the surface. Wipe off the dirt with a damp, tepid cloth.

Wearing the Mask

When wearing a mask do not stand stiff and motionless. An added lifelike quality is given by a slight movement of the head either from side to side or up and down. Shifting from foot to foot with body motion and using the arms and hands will add to the lifelike effect. Above all try as far as possible to conceal the back of the head.

If a mask is too large or the eye level is incorrect the fault may be corrected by stuffing a handkerchief between the top of the mask and the head.

In wearing a female mask if the wearer's hair is of a different color the hair should be pinned back.

When wearing a mask with a double chin, or impersonating a fat or short necked person hunch up the shoulders. A double chin in real life will stretch out when the head is raised. With a mask the chin remains immovable so keep the head down.

In a crowd or cocktail party it is best to keep close supervision over your mask or masks. A great many people do not know the value of a well made mask nor appreciate its fragility. Do not let a large headed person, a fat one with a double chin or one with an abundance of hair try to force a mask on that is too small. A split mask will result.

Most of the male masks shown in this book are worn by the author. The difference in their appearance demonstrates the wide variety of figures and personalities obtainable.

On Using Photographs

In modeling a portrait mask it is not unethical in this hectic world to use photographs. The more photographs obtainable of the subject the better. However, it is most essential that a straight front and side views with the same expression are used for the preliminary build-up. This saves hours of tiresome posing. When a likeness is built up as far as possible one sitting by your victim should be all that is necessary to make all necessary changes.

Remember that a photograph always lies. One print will bring out something entirely lacking in another. A third print will bring out some other feature because of different lighting.

Years ago cartoonist McCutcheon of the *Chicago Tribune* had printed a dozen photographs of a man in exactly the same pose for each one but each with a different lighting. Some of the pictures were not recognizable as the same man.

Photographs as a rule flatten out and do not show the bone structure of the forehead. Candid camera shots taken up close, front view, are apt to make the nose larger than it really is. In analyzing a photograph of a woman's face do not be fooled on the mouth structure by the artificial lines given to it by lip-stick.

Finish

It is surprising how rough in texture a mask can be. Actual skin is fairly rough. Many mask makers, in fabricating a naturalistic mask make the mistake of polishing the surface to a high finish. A too highly finished surface gives a hard, sharp half-tone. Witness the hard, metallic, unsympathetic smoothness of window display mannikins.

A fairly rough surface catches the light and carries it around the surface curves, gives it a wider halftone and gives a more pleasing and realistic texture.

Caricature

It is amazing how far one may depart from the truth in caricature and still maintain plausibility when the mask is worn in conjunction with the body. In caricaturing a mask is restricted by the necessity of making the eye holes come out right for good visibility by the wearer.

Do not overstep and make a caricature so violent it will seem impossible. Remember that the naturalistic and the unnaturalistic do not go well together. Many caricaturists emphasize the impossible. It is better to make an impossibility look possible.

The less a person is known the harder it is to caricature him. It takes years of constant publicity to establish in the public mind a sort of recognizable symbolism, such as certain characteristic eye glasses, teeth, jaw, moustache, hair, etc. It takes only the barest suggestions of some certain accessory to establish a likeness in the public's mind.

Some people lend themselves to caricature while others are almost impossible to do. One must have what Wm. Oberhardt, that master portraitist, calls a pump-handle face; there is something to grab ahold of. Obviously it is not in the realm of the caricaturist to make the negative into the positive. The artist has much more leeway as a caricaturist than has the sculptor.

Movie stars are a problem apart. Candid shots taken stepping out of a Pullman or airplane are often hardly recognizable. Stars are best known by their made up publicity stills. Here is one case where a photographic likeness supercedes an actual likeness . . . that is, in the minds of the public.

A pre-VJ Day conception

Other Methods

A Hollywood technician once remarked that the method employed here was the hard way. Perhaps it is, but the results may justify the means.

The best known and commercial way of making masks is the papier-mache method of pressing wet carpet paper into a plaster mold. The advantage of this method is that it allows for duplication. The disadvantages are that a plaster mold must first be made; the mold must be over simplified for easy removal of the mask; or the mold must be made into a highly intricate piece mold if those folds and planes that go to show character are to be retained.

Another drawback is that, to prevent buckling, the paper must be laid too thick and heavy for comfortable wearing later. If it is thick and heavy the mask has to be made larger if it is to be worn; larger than a form fitting one. Also the surface as a rule calls for much filling and treatment.

By the laminated method described in this book the model is destroyed in the making. This permits of but one mask being made and its value definitely enhanced.

The Case of the Life Mask

One would naturally think that a life mask would be the last word in likenesses. If well made even the pores of the skin show. Strange as it may seem very few life masks are satisfactory from a likeness standpoint or they would be more popular.

In the plaster process it may well be that the weight of the plaster pressing the flesh against the bony structure may have something to do with this but in other methods where weight is not a factor the results are about the same. Coloring or toning down the whiteness of the plaster helps somewhat but the real reason is something entirely different. This is that the merging of the planes are too subtle to catch the eye . . . are not simplified enough.

All this leads up to the importance of simplifications and caricature. The successful portrait artist or sculptor well knows that caricature gives character. Some people think that caricature means gross exaggeration. The secret of caricature is to not make the caricature obvious.

USES

Aside from the sheer fun to be had with a mask there is quite a field for practical exploitation. The making of a mask is much easier than finding the market for one. Returns from rentals far exceed sales.

Artists find masks a great help as models for the study of different lighting effects. Their use in masquerades is obvious.

Perhaps the best way to indicate the many ways in which a mask may be put to use is to give a partial list of the places and occasions where the author's masks have figured:

Masks have been shown and demonstrated before the National Press Club and Gridiron Banquet in Washington, D. C. Before the Salmagundi and Lotus Club, Cornell Club Reunion, Advertising Club of N. Y., Time-Life party, Woodstock Playhouse, Tuxedo Masonic Camp, Ohio Club and N. Y. Medico Surgical Society.

Lectures have been given before the Poor Richard Club, Phila., Art Directors Club, Finch College and five times before the Art School League of New York. Powell masks have been used in Harvard's Hasty Pudding Show, the Lambs Spring Gambol, Dutch Treat and Art Directors shows, Ringling Bros. Circus, Society of Illustrators shows (six times) and Billy Rose's Diamond Horseshoe (three years).

Movie shorts and newsreels: Paramount Pictorial, Fox, Pathe, MGM, Warner Bros., Universal and Columbia Pictures.

National Broadcasting has broadcast quite a few mask pictures while window displays, fashion and store displays have been given by Wanamaker, Macy's, Best & Co. in New York, T. Eaton Co. in Toronto, Canada, Marshall Field in Chicago and stores in Detroit, Los Angeles, Denver, San Francisco, Washington, D. C. and many other cities. Magazine and newspaper features have been shown in two-page spreads in Harpers Bazaar, Parade, Pic and Picture Wise. Full pages in the World Telegram, N. Y. and NEA Sunday Supplement. Illustrated articles in the Cosmopolitan, Look, New York Times, Journal-American, Mirror and in an Associated Press release, Coronet, Popular Science, Chicago Tribune Gravure. Abroad the London Sketch and Illustrated, London have given half-page features.

Window display at BEST & CO., 5th Ave., New York. Left to right: Garbo, Hepburn, Crawford, Harlowe and West.

Scene from a Paramount Pictorial showing left to right: Hepburn, Menjou, Robinson, West, Durante, Arliss, Al Smith, Gen. Johnson, W. C. Fields and Garner.

N.B.C. PHOTOS

Pictures taken in the N.B.C. television studio.
Left: Franklin D. Roosevelt. Upper right: Al Smith.
Lower right: Herbert Hoover while President.

These pictures reproduced in New York Times and Popular Science.

David Workman Photo

Peter Donald (not a mask), raconteur preeminent, shakes
hands with the author representing Pres. Truman.

At a Time-Life party a large blow-up was made of the front page cover of TIME. Through a
hole cut in the cover, guests were photographed with the character of their choice.

Katherine Hepburn

Owned by artist Neysa McMein

In photographing a head it helps to have an appropriate costume in keeping with the character.
If possible put a young face on a youthful body, a more mature face on an older body. Here
10¢ store ear-rings are wired on.

Winston Churchill

Senator McNary

This and the three following pages show that the mask can be considered seriously as a medium for portraiture.

General Knudson

Sloan of General Motors

Portrait mask of Wallace Morgan, Honorary President
of the Society of Illustrators.

Owned by the Society

James Montgomery Flagg
A portrait mask of the noted illustrator
owned by the Lotos Club, N. Y.

72

H. V. Kaltenborn
Portrait of the radio commentator made
with the help of pencil sketches.

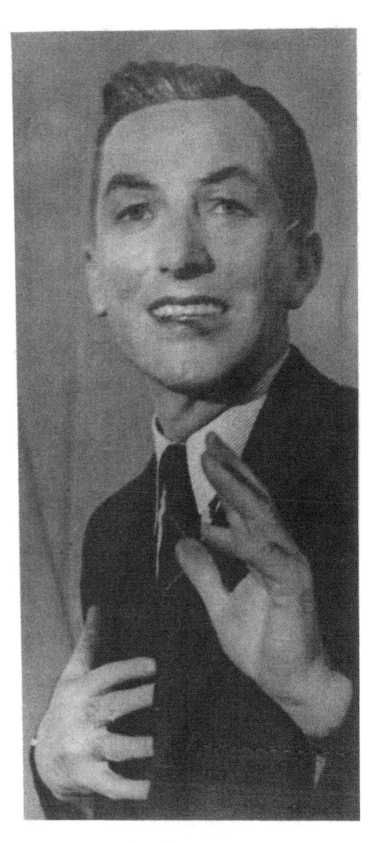

Lanny Ross
Made with the aid of pencil sketches

Owned by Mr. Ross

CHARACTER MELANGE

Never underestimate the value of a smile.

QUIPS ON REMOVING A MASK

"I got ahead of him that time."
"That's how to get ahead."
"Just think of my overhead."
"Here's a little face lifting."
"You go on ahead. I'll stay and face it."
"Don't call me two faced."

Self portrait.   *Wendell MacRae Photo*

THAT'S ALL